CW00842291

NAKED

NAKED

'Speak' they tell me 'You can speak to me'.
    And yet I cannot. Believe me, I have tried.
    I have held my tongue for so many years, I have
    forgotten how to let it go.

I searched through the ends of my memories to find
where it was that I let myself go.
I looked through every bar and restaurant.
Through the spine on my pen and diary.
Through every tear in my bed and pillow.
I searched through the ends of my memories to find
where it was that I lost myself.
In each smile and laugh of the photographs on my
phone, I found a girl broken. I found unheard tears and
pain, unseen fear. I found a girl unwanted with a heart
full of words unspoken.

All she ever wanted was for someone to hear what she
had to say. She was on the verge of an explosion.

The constant pressure to be like my mother.
To conform to society
To be oppressed by men
To speak low
To internalize my thoughts
She has taught me
Silence.

I have wanted to die on many moons but none have been as brutal as the ones caused by my mother

I am trying
But I am so tired.
I am trying
But all I am left with is myself, worn out, soaking my sheets
with gallons of saltwater.

I watch as my father digs in his pocket to pay for my overpriced birthday gift. I turn away and pretend I do not hear the coins chink in his pockets. I pretend I do not hear him haggling for a cheaper price. I sink and crawl in embarrassment that we cannot afford the gift as well as pay for supper. But I see the determination in his body; in the way he speaks to the man until he gets his way. I thank him but I cannot look him in his eyes because I feel ashamed that I have been selfish. In all my years of living, I have never seen my father celebrate his birthday. He says he does not remember when he was born yet I see the dates marked boldly on his identification card and birth certificate. He makes sure we have a birthday to remember but insists that we must never celebrate his.

Sacrifice

I am afraid that what I speak is never important
Constantly at war with being myself

I feel abandoned
I feel left alone
I feel uncared for
I feel lacking
I feel judged
I feel uninteresting
I feel like I always have to try harder
I feel like I have to assert my strength
I feel like I need to make people listen
I feel like people make assumptions of who I am
I feel like I have to prove to people that I am kind
I feel alone.

I got intoxicated and spoke of the feelings I could not reveal when I was sober.

I am overcome with unsettling thoughts.
　　My future.
　　My career.
　　My family.
　　My needs.
　　Money.
　　...
　　Each thought manifests into an image.
　　...
　　Bright colours.
　　Sunshine.
　　Flowers.
　　Life.
　　...
　　Each image weaves into the next, perfectly
　　sketched.
　　Money is the artist.

The heavy realization that money defines all of my
dreams.

She was brave and strong and fierce, unafraid of
anything.
And she took life by the neck and made it hers. But the
only thing that made her human was the only thing she
was most scared of.

Her feelings.

Born and raised in the motherland, I have witnessed utilization of our recourses by everyone. I have seen countries and co-operations invite themselves to the table. To feast like the farmers that ploughed in the summer and the herders that watched over the cattle they so proudly feast upon. I have seen organisations replace the hosts and invite their counterparts while the hosts eat in the kitchen and serve fine wine from vineyards. As I walk down the streets of my hometown, I can see the oppression of my people. In their eyes, in their tired faces and dusty feet. In the way they march the town looking for jobs that do not exist.

I am a foreigner in a country I have come to call home.
But the borders do not care for my feelings.

When mothers do not want to understand
When mothers do not want to listen
It is betrayal so deep that life itself is no longer worth living

I close my eyes and lay on my newly washed sheets. Aromas of lavender invade my nostrils and caress my hairs, as I inhale a deep breath to put to rest the day and give way to the night. I am at peace…I am content. I take a moment to relax and bask in the presence of God, as I humbly seek Him to give thanks… but the atmosphere has shifted. I lay, still as a sculpture, as my ears enlarge to capture the unfamiliar sounds. My nose follows in collaboration breathing softly, and gently, as if counselling my heart to stay calm. The atmosphere has shifted. I rub my eyes in hopes that my imagination is running wild and let my vision come to life in a sudden awakening, only to find myself in a world I do not understand. My breathing accelerates, louder and heavier as if gasping for my last breath. My eyes shut themselves tightly, refusing to see what was unfolding in front of them. My feet take heed behind my hips and my thighs curl up to my breast holding on for dear life. My arms, so quick to think, construct a halo around my shins. I opened my eyes…only to discover myself in a state of numbness. Time became void, as tears showered the soft skin on my face. I lay there helpless and watched.

I watched myself in a state of panic about a man that never deserved to know me the way I allowed him to. I watched as I lost control.

I wanted to pick myself up and hold me. I wanted to give myself the world, the moon, the sun, her stars, and the flowers. I stared at my big brown eyes and heavy shoulders. I was terrified. I screamed at myself, pinching and beating my thighs and biting my arms as if this pain was better than whatever had crept inside.

And then something...a miracle. I felt my arms unravel, as if the glue holding them around my shins had been softened. Then my thighs began to peep out of their shell to examine the safety of the room. My feet not too far behind stretched their little helpers across the sheets...My body awoke from its slumber and assembled its components, ready to reconstruct. Time began to move. My lungs conducted the operation, dusting off the cobwebs around my kidneys and built a ladder to the edge of my nostrils. My windpipe, stretched its fingers and picked the scattered pieces of my heart and glued them together. And slowly the sobbing and the screaming hushed and came to a still silence.

~NAKED~

What do you want from me?
'Intimacy' I replied
To feel. To connect. To listen with my heart, mind, body and soul.

The time I loved a man that only wanted my body.

I am clay and saltwater
I am milk and honey
But today...
Today feels like 6ft deep and a casket.

I have watched myself lose fragments of my mind
    to undeserving men.
    to unappreciative friends.
And I have wept as I watched the pieces float across the sky
and disappear with memories both sweet and painful.

In the night when everyone is asleep, I stay awake watching the cracks in the ceiling of my room leaking heavy brown water into the edge of my bed. The silence of the dark makes me uneasy, unworthy, inadequate. It comes with it the crackling of the heat radiating from the light bulb, the company of heavily loaded lorries swerving off the nearby highway, and the chaos of the thoughts in my mind.

In the morning my father bangs on my door not knowing my mind haunted me all night and has yet to go to sleep. He swings the door open yelling, 'you sleep too much' but I do not even remember what that means.

I am grateful for the loud in the house when my brother awakes and talks to himself in the shower, when my sister sings aloud outside my room when my mother begins to make her porridge and turns the radio on as she bangs the pots and pans against each other. When the birds begin to croak, and not sing, when the sun burns and not shines into my window.

I am grateful when the haunting, chaotic, quiet of the night comes to an end and the sounds of dawn bring about disruption. This is when I find peace. This is when I go to sleep.

Broken.

As the sun looked over me throughout my birthdays, my mother taught me about my thick hair, my wide nostrils and my round lips. She rubbed the sun on my skin as the song in my bones played and I danced until dusk just so I could remember what she looked like. I failed to speak as she taught me, elongating my vowels aggressively almost viciously attacking my consonants to mean exactly what I say. I am ashamed of failing to acknowledge my mother, who sacrificed her legs so I could walk back home when mine could no longer carry me.

> To the time I denounced Africa as my mother.

It is too loud to go outside, I cannot hear myself. But it is too quiet to stay inside, I can hear too much of myself

And when the chaos of the heavy winds break the windows of the small café and the ground opens up and swallows the buildings, I will sit there with a cup of black coffee and I will close my eyes and breathe. The smell of roasted coffee will linger in the air and into my nostrils and the instruments in the radio will serenade my ears as if the melodies were written just for me. I will sit in the middle of that café until the fire falling from the clouds consumes the walls of the room. I will smile and sip the last of my coffee just as the instruments in the radio come to an end, as the deep waters from the ocean rush into the streets and sweep me off my seat.

And the familiar feeling of hopelessness will disappear into thin air.

So tight were the walls,
she sacrificed her heart just to get out
He was supposed to be the one,
everybody saw it. A match made in heaven.
When she read his letter, her words curled up behind her
throat
and rolled down to her stomach to keep company
her knotted dreams and dotted hopes.
Her neglected young heart slowed until
praying became a chore.

On March 1st.
When the stranger in the bus decided to... I let him.
I let him caress my arms as he wished because my stomach
formed those dancing butterflies that it used to whenever
the boy I liked touched my thighs.
WAS I UNCOMFORTABLE?
Of course, I was.
I had never felt such discomfort in my life.
But I let him... I let him slip his hand inside my skirt.
WHY DIDN'T I DO ANYTHING?
Well... I was scared
I thought that no one would have believed me.
But I let him... I let him slide his hand over my womanhood.
WHY DIDN'T I STOP HIM?
... I froze
I thought they would have attacked me.
I thought they would have said I was asking for it.
But it's true, I let him... I let him take advantage of that dark
night.
I SHOULD HAVE SCREAMED?
Well...
The letters ran and hid in the depth of my stomach.
My throat became dry and the words refused to leave my
mouth.
My eyes locked themselves shut and refused to identify his
face.
My hands wrapped themselves around my breasts and
refused to move his away.
WHY DIDN'T I LEAVE?

The bus was moving.
I was sat up against the window.
We were in the middle of nowhere, in the middle of
the night.
But those are not the only reasons
My legs hid behind the seat and refused to come back
to me.
HOW DO I FEEL?
Well...
I let him...
On March 1st
When the stranger on the bus decided to come in...
Did I let him?

We stared at each other.
That purple bottle of cough syrup and I.
She wanted me and I wanted her and we both wanted to
end.
Both our lives.
Hers in me
Mine on the cold floor of my room.

I wanted them to find me in the morning.
To knock on my door until the hinges undid themselves
To find me lying on the hard ground with 2 bottles of wine
and an empty bottle of cough syrup.
A note: To all the mothers that raised me, I am free.

There is something about the voices
The ones in my head that want me to stop
The ones that want me to listen
They keep talking at me.
They cannot stand it when I approach the finish line.
They nag me to stop.
They care way too much
Most times, they don't care enough.
They are worried.
They are uncomfortable.
A little scared that I will fail.
A little nervous that I am trying
But those voices, way too many voices
Are no longer allowed in my premises.

I heard those words pierce through my eyes
prickling like thinned needles.
I blinked.
Once, twice, thrice, four times hoping by the fifth,
I would believe it.
I looked up and down
on his cheeks and his neck,
his feet and forehead
everywhere but his eyes ashamed
that he would see the lie that leaked through the
weight of my breath.
My toes and fingers danced out of beat
then curled up like they had been trying to escape the
ordeal.
'You are so beautiful!'
The man that I had dreamed of for many moons
approached and grabbed my hand
'You are so beautiful!'
Those words pierced through to my core
hard-hitting like a heavy blow to my stomach.
Cool air rushed in through my lips into my mouth
and pushed against the poetry that I had been
rehearsing for weeks.
I watched as he waited
and waited and waited for my response
but my legs had already assessed the situation and
lifted me in haste to the bathroom.
I stumbled into the cubicle and all that poetry pushed
out of my mouth

forcing itself up my throat and down the sink in
thick liquid.
My hands wrapped themselves around my waist
as I dropped down to my knees and howled like a
hundred tired wolves.
I had been many things in my lifetime
but beautiful had never been one of them.

On good days, there is sunshine. I keep busy. I stay productive. I do my laundry and use the lavender scented fabric softener. I listen to Fela Kuti and dance to the beats of his saxophone. I sway left, right, spin around then salsa and samba and play my imaginary drums and all the while, my skin absorbs the sunlight. I sit out in the open air and observe the blue sky, birds flying high, the insects with their buzzing settling on pink and purple flowers. I close my eyes and listen to the whistles in the wind. I can hear the trees singing to accompany the diverse sounds. La vie en rose. But I can't help it.

I think of the hours in bed, unopened curtains, unwashed sheets, remnants of food scattered on the carpet. When the voices are too loud. When the winds laugh and snicker at me, when the singing of the trees sounds like croaking toads, when the sun burns my eyes and the blue sky turns grey. The birds high above pick on me and the insects with their aggressive buzzing aim to sting at me.

But I can't help but think that all good things come to an end.

I heard of the sunshine that lit up the sky from dawn to dusk. The kind of sunlight that made everybody laugh under the mango trees with bottles of cold coca colas and home-baked mandazis.

I heard of the farmers with pieces of land that spread out on the rough earth wide enough to cover the distance of the sea above.

I heard of the flowers that sung tales of gratitude and joyous carols all year long.

I heard of blue waters that welcomed the people and cleansed their souls.

Cool breezes and sweet waves that formulated plateaus and hills and low mountains in the crystals of the waters

Thousands of flamingos across the lakes dancing and swaying and playing and it was a happy time.

I heard of the same town, buildings shot up in the sky like rockets, disrupting the serenity of the scene.

I heard that the flamingos had left to seek a more deserving home outside of the chaos that was unfolding.

I heard the flowers shrivelled up like old men in the winter.

 I heard that the green leaves of the dancing trees had turned yellow and brown and sucked off all their juices until they fell to the ground, and the men and women and children who sat under the shade that once was walked over the rotten fruits and tossed them in a furnace of garbage.

So I packed my things and I went to see.

I saw the sun shining down like in the olden tales, but the mango trees were dry and the people under the half-hearted shade were no longer laughing.

Their faces twisted as if the gods they believed in had abandoned them.
I saw men and women and children wake before dawn, and drag their feet for miles in dusty unattended roads to fend for themselves and their families.
I saw them argue on the streets pushing each other against matatu doors like someone owed them something.
The wide lake had dried up to the last speck of sand, and wild dogs and cats chased each other up and down where the flamingos once danced, and swayed, and played to the beats of the town.
The cool breezes had turned brown, flying into the town with dust and chaff attacking the people's vibandas (kiosks) with no remorse
As tears fell from the sky, heavy, salty, tired tears, the town yelled, cried, screamed for anyone to listen.
There was a time when the sun shone so brightly over the sky from dawn to dusk.
 A time when the sunlight made everybody laugh under the mango trees with bottles of cold coca colas and home-baked mandazis.
Where did those days go?
Isn't it strange?

I return to the place where once before was too loud to go outside and too loud to stay inside.
Once upon a time I was attacked by sounds too broad to grasp.
They congregated in my mind like an angry mob in town hall and begun a revolution too powerful to stand my ground.
They pulled my ears from within and established control.
WHO AM I?
It is packed!
My seat up on the steps is unoccupied as if they knew I was coming.
Memories of the past come flooding in as I sit on the flesh coloured seats.
BREATHE.
It is too loud outside and too loud inside yet today the noises sniffed me out as I walked in through the doors and fled far, left hanging, peering through the cracked glasses of the windows.

Growth

It is neither happy nor sad, dry nor wet. It is neither light nor dark, summer nor fall. It is neither me nor you.

Yes.

Love conquers all.

but
        have
                you
                        ever
                                had
                                        consistent
                        communication
                with

        someone
you
        love
                ?

Saturday came and I waited for his call. Each hour checking my phone to make sure I wouldn't miss it. Hours turned into days and I started to wonder if he had been so busy. He said he worked night shifts so maybe he was just tired. So I left him a message. Days turned into weeks and nothing. I hoped that something had happened to him because it was better than believing I had been ghosted for the second time. Maybe he hadn't had the chance to make contact. I felt nauseous at every possibility that could explain it. So I called him. As the tone on the phone got louder, I heard my heart pounding trying to escape. I held on tightly when a voice came on the phone, 'I'm sorry, but the person you are trying to reach, is on another call, you can leave a message after the beep...' I stayed hopeful as the days turned weeks and into months...I was still waiting.

Unrequited love

I thought I would experience love when I found someone to love me.
I found you and lost myself in a sea of your kisses and in the warmth of your embrace, only for you to leave me in a storm of painful winds and tearful raindrops.
I gave you more love than you could handle.

Was that wrong of me?

All this so that a man can feel comfortable?

GIRL, PLEASE!

I have wanted to die so many times but

....

Precious Lord!

I am sorry that my demons were too much for you.

I am so many faces.
A culmination of
who I want to be
who I used to be
who I think I am
And who I become when I am with you

Nobody is talking. My teeth pull up and down like
a tug of war. The light dims, the rain begins to
pour, the music is fading, the knives in my throat
hold me hostage, the soldiers in my stomach
charge towards the wall, my feet clench and my fist
is against the temple of my face.
His presence is heavily felt. I see him standing
broad, laughing, smoking, smelling like everything
but me.
And as the music fades and my eyes undo
themselves my body releases and gravity cannot
stop pulling the salt from my eyes.

When I see you, I am different
When I leave you, I leave me.
She becomes my thoughts
Creeps in my fingertips and crawls beneath my skin
She lives in me but she is not me
That woman that leaves her scent on your body
Caresses her skin on yours
Undresses you with her thighs and eyes.
Her.
Tell her I want myself back
And I don't ever want to see you again
...
Who even are you?!

When the wind blows
We wish we were wrapped in sacks of cotton
that our crying hearts were enclosed in furnaces that our
feet were deep under the thick materials of our blankets.
When the rains pour
we run and hide behind heavy metal and wood
we cover our bodies under layers of clothing
we arm ourselves with convincing stories of why he did what
he did.
But today, is different.
I welcome the rough winds and let it swoosh across my face
in hopes that the voices that sing and curse in the chaos will
smack a thousand senses back to me.
I let the winds carry my baggage and bring back in tattered
scrolls all the times I called you just to say I love you in 7
different languages.
I beg the winds to search for my tired heart from wherever it
is that I left it.
And for a moment it feels possible.
I feel a whirl of liberty swimming in the pool of my blood.
My arms unravel from their shell and go up to dance with
the whoosh of the wind so I look up to the sun and let it
caress my skin and ease me into my long-awaited freedom.
And I dance and smile and sing along to the voices that sing
and curse in the chaos of the wind.
...Until the rays begin to burn and a hundred hot rods land
on my body.

The 7 languages of love turn into whips and lashes stripping away his scent from my existence.

    Today, when the wind blows, I will carry my sorrows and hide them in sacks of cotton so that when I lie down in the comfort of my bed, I will always be reminded of the man whose words snatched the poetry out of my lips.

Dinner got cold as she waited furiously for him; only to be met with the realisation that she had legs.
And she got up and walked away with a smile to fend for herself.

A false move,
and I will leave you asking the crickets which direction I
ran off to.

Her love was awakened by the soft in his lips
Winds uttered with much thought yet none at all
He spoke with the experience of many darkened cheeks
and many lonely hips and crooked smiles and searching
faces.
Young boy had mastered the art of finesse
 A curve of his tongue released a field of roses, boxes of
chocolates, long walks at the beach, a stolen dance in a
neighbourhood in the South of Spain
Late night conversations that left her eyes swollen, her
cheeks paralysed, her spine fractured.
A slip of his finger down the break of her back and letters of
poetic justice dripped to the cracks in her thighs.
Colours of the young artiste painted her brown canvas
where yellow became green and orange became teal
From the strands in her hair to the polish on her feet, she
was the poem.
That morning, the sun rose in the south and set behind the
trees in her neck.
That night, the stars splattered like knots and crosses in-
between the clouds and the moon landed on the man.
Her tongue was the nose and her eyes became her hands,
her feet her stomach and her ears became her tears.
Young boy had mastered the art of finesse.

I am tired of loving like a prisoner in my own home

WAKE UP!
The sun stretches out its claws and pounces on her face
screaming,
yelling,
aggressively,
tragic
the darkness laid in comfort underneath her eyes.
WAKE UP!
She sits on her bed covered in
Stings
and
scratches
and
bites.
A culmination of a love that wrapped itself in honey-coated
lips, sweet caresses and lengthy hugs that turned the world
from bottles of spiced rum to sweet cocktails.
both a little bitter
both a little toxic
both a little comfort
both a little cosy.
Both turned her freezing Mondays into warm Sunday
afternoons.

You taught me how to love
I never knew what that looked like
And then my legs carried me to another
And I felt sure.
For my eyes were meant for him
And my lips kept asking for his
And I felt selfish
But I had never felt so alive.

I wish I had expressed that when I spoke to you, my chest unlocked a convoy of drawers locked away in a fear of being everything other than myself.

When you found your way to my table, I stayed away from you and avoided your gaze because I knew what those beautiful eyes of yours could do to me.

When I spoke to you, it was as if God had been writing His script for our existence and our scene had been so perfectly constructed, nothing could falter.

We knew our lines even though this was the very first time we had met.

And we talked and talked until the hot air turned into cold winds.

We talked until our mouths ran dry, until the words no longer spewed out of our mouths so naturally.

We searched for ourselves in each sentence, each word, each letter.

And when the setting of the dancing trees, the singing wind and the adlibs of the voices of children, men and women came to a standstill, the world stopped for us.

It was like we had found ourselves in all those sentences, words and letters.

It is as if we found more than we were looking for in each other's eyes, fingers, lips.

We found something wonderfully wrapped up in the chaos of our hearts, of our minds and our souls.

We found our perfect match in each other's words.

My flowers and butterflies could not bear to reveal
their secret.
When he asked to hear my love poem...
Rivers began to overflow from the depth of my eyes,
Paste like porridge, sipped through my mouth and lay it
shut. My lips bounced against each other like fish sipping
the ocean at night. I began to undo his fingers on my
cheeks, his gaze from my eyes. I stretched my hand to my
chest and pulled out my heart from its disguise. My iris tried
to memorise his writing on my skin but my fingers quickly
plucked any traces of him out of the pottery. Because I was
certain he would leave knowing the ugly secret I kept from
him. It was his lips that should have been painted on the
pages of that poem. I could not bear to hear his voice when
I told him that I was sorry.
Sorry that when he found me searching in the
wilderness, he chose me.
Sorry that I was saving another man just as he reached
out to rescue me.
Sorry that another man has accumulated that part of
the poem that belonged to him.
Sorry that I should have told you, you were not the only
one.

January 2nd. When he asked to hear my love poem... My
flowers and butterflies could not bear to reveal their secret.

I am tired of hearing I love you with nothing to show for it.

Perhaps our time has passed. Maybe, it has not yet come. But I must go, I am in need of getting out.

Breakup| Breakout| Break-free

Each morning I wake up to the melody of familiar birds and compose a sweet poem for you. At night, when the singing birds have returned and the owls haunt the neighbourhood, I write poems that turn organic honey into tequila.

LOML

Catch me in the morning.
when the day has not yet done its work on me.
Find me in the depths of the night.
when the day has finished taking its toll on me.
.

My naked truth,
It will paint your body like a Matisse canvas
My writing,
It will spill my sonnets on the pages of your lips
.

Seek for me, let us
dance to the beats of our hearts
to the pitch of our mourns
to the tones in our breaths
.

Come.
Let us sing with our bodies this duet,
like the Nyatiti has been cultivating in our blood.

Stop apologising for your broken English.
Yes, it is different.
Yes, it is attractive.
Yes, I am in love with your sounds.
English is not the language of your origin my love.

My son,
You talk of being hard because society expects you to.
Because this is what makes you a real man.
Your sister cries in her bedroom each night because of a
man. This 'man' swears he is a real man because he is
hard. I ask you what is so wrong about vulnerability?
You express with aggression and scoff in my face that it
is not what a man should be. it is soft. it is gay.

But I see it in your eyes that this hard-ness has beaten
you to your knees. I can see the bags in your eyes
sagging low, carrying the burden of your perception of
manhood. But that is all you have ever been and you do
not know where to begin to return, reposition, retouch
and relearn how to be a man.

My son,
I am sorry that I did not teach you any better. Sometimes,
our culture hinders our individuality. Let the sun radiate
from your skin and let those flowers blossom from your
chest. Do not let society tell you who to be and how to
be. Dig deep and find out who you really are. Go and be
your heart's desires.
        Your vulnerability will give way to your manhood.

I am sorry that you have never had the love that I am giving you. Perhaps, it may be too much. I have penetrated your walls but you have quickly found a mason to rebuild them and put me off. You turn away and tell me that I am incapable of fixing you, that I will be broken if I remain with you. I am sorry that my love is too much for you.

But know that when your souls sings, mine joins in harmony. When your heart dances, mine choreographs the steps. When your mind sketches a picture, mine paints in between the lines. But when your soul is lost, mine brings the flashlight. When your heart is shattered, mine collects the pieces. When your mind is flooded, mine begins to rebuild a new home.

You are me and I am you. Let me give you comfort and warm up those parts of you stuck in winter.
You have been for me the light at the end of the tunnel on many moons. I promised to shelter, protect and take care of you. I could never leave. My conscience would never forgive me.

Your man is not superhuman.
He too needs ice cream and TLC.

I look for you.
    in the pain in my chest
    in the confusion of my thoughts.
    In the whistle in the wind
    in the aromas in my house.
    The corners of my eyes
    In the creases of my palm.
    ...
In the morning you send me your love and confess that you have wanted me.
I want to see your eyes when you say this. I want to hold your hand, feel your spirit and read you from the lines on your feet to the strands on your head.
But I cannot.
I weep because my heart longs for one touch.
I break because I can no longer bear to be with you without being with you.

Long-distance relationship

I want to write a thousand and one poems about
the colour of your eyes.
From sunrise when I can
barely see through the thickness
of your married lashes to midday
when the sun returns the hazel to your eyes to
sunset
when the sky confesses her love for you
and our eyes undress each other into the horizon...

You have always been the mediator of my thoughts. My demons are quieter with you. You have always negotiated my position in this war.

I love you.

For his lips craved the sunshine in her back,
He went exploring and found life untouched.
unopened letters
unread messages
undiscovered truths
unhealed promises.
He grabbed his tools and opened the unopened
letters, read the unread messages and found a
million more written in braille.
It would take him 90 days and 90 nights to complete
the first.
Only 999,999 more to go.
His fingers spooning each one softly, kindly,
lovingly, patiently.
He began his journey
For his lips craved the sunshine in her back.

Here I am, draped in silk, wrapped around the arms of the love of my life. I wish that I could never wake up.

I wish you taught me your language and I taught you mine when you were still here.

I miss you.

I dreamt of us on Tuesday night. We sat in our apartment; you, reading a magazine and I, writing my poems. We gazed at each other constantly because our spirits could not bear to be without each other. I knew you were my soul mate because I dreamt the same dream last night. We were 80 years old and we were writing a memoir of our love. You gazed at me and I was instantly filled with peace. And then I came to you and slipped under your arms and we both rested in each other's warmth.

Through the thick fog,
I watch planes fly above the heads of the houses in
my neighbourhood. I smile when I imagine that its
destination is your location then I cry a little because
I wish I was flying through those smoky clouds to
come and see you.
I love you through the miles that are too tall to
climb.
I wish that every mountain was a gateway to your
front door so I could go hiking and disappear into
the woods like Alice
to discover a wonderland that is you and me.
I love you through the airwaves on my phone. When
I wish I was more than a picture on your screen so
you could touch me like you do when you zoom into
my lips and double-tap my thighs. So that I could
feel your fingertips when you touch the essence of
my skin though my words are too subtle and
sometimes too broad to encapsulate how I feel
about you and me and us.
I LOVE YOU.
Though I have never said those words to you.
I am scared that you will hold on to its essence until
the mud is wiped off your eyes and you see me.
Lost and Anxious.
Hurt and Broken.
and you will tear my love with disgust smeared on
your tired lips and cast it out into dusty winds to fly
back to me.

Tattered and Uprooted
Scattered and Removed.
And yet, I will still love you.
Hopelessly
Wholeheartedly
Romantically
Fearlessly.

I walked away because he had poisoned my thoughts and I was determined to undo his fingers, his lips, his breathe on my person just so I could find my way back to you, lighter, better, happier.
I walked away because you deserve the universe and all its stars and all I had been able to give you was broken seashells and washed out pebbles.

STOP. BREATHE. BE.

You are allowed to be lost
To be broken.
To be angry
To scream, shout and cuss.
To let your pain burst out.
You are allowed to stay in bed. To be sad and
to cry and to hold on to your pillow.
To seek comfort in cheesy spaces

You are allowed to be broken.

You lose a piece of yourself each time you try to be who you are not.

The one will never come to you
If you never come to yourself.

No matter where I go, I carry my people, my culture, my traditions. On the strength of my grip, the depth in my sight, the darkness of my skin, the texture of my hair and in the cracks of my feet.
My culture and my traditions have been in me since before my soul found my body in my mother's womb.

Now that I am sunshine, I am soft, I am loved. I lust, care, cry, feed, fall madly in love and tend to myself.

Now that I am sunshine, I am my own relationship.

Become your biggest fan. Become your saviour.
And when you do not remember these two, know that
God is cheering you on. He will pick you up and remind
you of your worth.

There are unspoken fears and uncultivated treasures only you have access to. No one can be you better than you.

Why do you change your nose to look like another's,
your lips to look like someone you have never met, your
breasts to take up an unnatural shape?
 You even wash out your skin with acid to erase the
 depth of the sun in your bones!

                                    You are art. Not the painter

If you never had the money to change yourself, would you still love yourself?

When it happens...
It's weighty.
A little mind-blowing.
A little exciting.
A little overwhelming.
A whole lotta warmth and happy in your soul.
And a deep sense of curiosity to discover more of
everything that has been hiding in you.

To fall in love with yourself will become a mission that will be impossible to abort.

To which I heard a voice, ' The gap between your vision
and ever seeing it, is God.'

Prayer

Forgive them and then forgive yourself
Go outside, embrace the clouds and take in a deep breathe
Then exhale and let the chaos in your mind float out into the air
Relax your forehead, drop your shoulders, release your stomach and keep breathing allowing the air to reach every part of your being
Straighten your back and let your head sit above your spine like a crown
Then repeat:

'I do not owe anyone anything.'

It could never just be light.
Life would be too dull.
Even the sun has to give way to rain
Day has to give way to dusk
Because we love, we have to grieve.

I am only responsible for saving myself. No one else is important when I am drowning.

Expressing yourself.
In Writing
In Speaking
In Whispers
In Song
In Crying
In Screaming
In Punching
In Dance
In Painting
In Walking
In Dreaming
In Loving

...

As long as you are allowing your feelings and those thoughts both ugly and beautiful to breathe...

You owe it to yourself to be Selfless.

The first love of your life MUST be you.

     Selflessness, not Selfishness.

Love takes different forms.
I Love God, myself, my family.
Love is not always about a man.

Stop being afraid of confirming your position in someone's life.

Be Vocal.
Ask Questions.
Speak.

Stop playing your uniqueness for him to see that you are different. He is not interested.
Work on your gifts. Work on your passion.
The one who deserves you will see all of you.

98

YOURS is YOURS.
YOUR life is YOURS and only YOURS to live.
Do not let anyone tell YOU how to live it.

It's about YOU. Period.

Ashes to ashes, dusk to voluptuous hips. She strolled down the streets. Hands free like she finally finished pulling colonisation out of her skin.
Eyes left to right turning like big wheels keep turning on highways.
Tip tap was the sound of her heels. Patterns so artistic and ancestral, she commanded their full attention. She smiled, she waved, like the goddess of her destiny.

She was an African woman in a Western country.

A woman scorned does not have to seek revenge.
A woman scorned can look the other way and work
on herself.

Someone else's path to success might be the road to your downfall.

Stop following narratives.

Every month.
the moon and the oceans deliberate to summon me.
they pull the walls of my stomach and press down
the dimples on my back.
I emit my digestion out of my front and back.
and the nerves in my head
Break
and reconstruct.
Break.
reconstruct.
Break
...
Calm
Tired
Strong
Pain
Nauseous
Insomnia
Pain
...
diamonds from my eyes cleanse my tight skin.
Blood trickles down my thighs
Clots
Heavy
Thick
Clumps
...
I am saltwater.
I am the tides in the ocean.

I am the moon in the darkness.
I am woman.

I have been corrected all my life.

That's not how you say that.
You are placing emphasis on the wrong words.
I can still hear your native tongue piercing through.
.

I have been corrected all my life to speak like
someone I am not.

I cannot understand what you are saying.
Your accent is too thick. You should speak softer.
You need to speak properly if you want to get the
job.
.

The white man invaded our land and killed our
people so he could rule over us. He introduced his
way of life and banished ours so he could understand
our intentions by making his language the official
one.
He comes to bask in the sun of our countries and asks
the shopkeeper if he can speak English yet when I go
to his home and ask the shopkeeper if he can speak
Swahili, I am told to learn the language or go back to
my country.

All my life, the white man has wanted me to speak
like him as if the world revolves around his language.

You can no longer colonise me/ I will finish you before you press your ideas on my people again/ this is Africa and you will tread on our terms.

Decolonising.

I do not have to explain myself to anyone hence I can never fix my lips to apologise for being myself.
                                             That is suicide.

The aromas of sweet pineapples and mangoes and tangerines in overcrowded markets.
The yellow and orange skies when the sun sets and rises.
The serene sounds of the birds at dawn curious outside our windows.
The touts persistently persuading you to ride with them and the hawkers knocking at your car window to buy roasted nuts and home-baked crisps.
I am learning to appreciate the simplicity in my life.

The conventions of life are very peculiar. The "pleases" and the "thank yous" as in the pleasing just to say thank you. We're constantly fighting to win people's affection yet we constantly lose against ourselves. We acquit ourselves with the rules and regulations of what we type and send on our screens. Going above and beyond for multiple likes, double taps, pleasing comments, favourites and the ability to uphold a status in a digital world. Our minds travel and discover the home of perfectionism and it overpowers our bodies. We become perfect and stride with pride. But perfectionism cannot coexist with our true selves. To be perfect, we investigate and question ourselves until we lose ourselves. We begin to feel inadequate but at least everyone knows we are perfect. We stink of a façade and our organs begin to rot, but at least everyone knows we are perfect. Our mouths begin to burn, unable to say what we feel but at least... Then at night our hands lose stability and shake with fear as we post a throwback picture, in memory of who we once were. Once upon a time you took off to find yourself, and on the way you found a loophole that led you to perfection. You took it. And failed to realise that perfection is more than you need and less than you can encapsulate. Today your mind creates a billion universes. Each one, a déjà vu, a reminder of you. But it is too late and you can hardly remember. You struggle to revive yourself but you have been long gone. You can never be the same again. Your imperfection had been perfect all along and now you cannot distinguish yourself from the person that exists on that screen.

Your purpose on earth has never been to find perfection. You are human, not artificial intelligence.

Trust what people show you more than what they tell you.
   Actions will always speak louder than words.

Do not integrate movie life into your love life
    You will always be disappointed. Trust me, I have tried.

Stop waiting for your knight in shining armour and fall in love with the person in the mirror.
Genuinely and
Unconditionally.

A land of milk and honey
I am that land of milk and honey

I am taking myself out to lunch today
We're going to talk about the weather
And life, and politics and drink fine wine
We will talk about us and him and love
And we will laugh and dance and drink fine wine
And it will be a great day

Me to Me: I could never live without you

Me to Me: You are my heart, my soul, my mind

Me to Me: You are the woman of my dreams.

I will love you
Across the seas and the oceans
Over the mountains and the treetops
I will love you
To the edge of the world and back
But I will still never love you as much as I love me

I love you but quite frankly, I do not like you.

True freedom is in accepting and loving who you are.
Wholeheartedly.

All my life I have been called the colour of midnight.
That I am 2am. Too dark to be seen at all.
That I am white teeth and eyeballs in the night.
...
Like this is a bad thing.

When you compare yourself to people, you gain nothing but unnecessary sadness and feelings of worthlessness.

It is not YET your time.
Breathe.
Give thanks.
The blessings that God is about to shower you with is still
brewing.

Neither man nor woman was created to be alone.

REACH.

Stop going back you are interrupting your progress.

Give yourself the time to understand who you are. Relax. Stop trying to impress everybody.

How people treat you is a reflection of how they treat
themselves.
It is not personal.

Focus your energy on being married to yourself. Love and treat yourself with so much love that when a man comes along, you know that you can already give yourself all that he is trying to offer you.

Beware of those people who never give you the support but are always the first to ask how you did it. They want assurance that you could never have done it on your own. That someone had to hold the door for you. Someone had to hold your shoes while you extended your feet. Someone had to do the work for you.

These people do not like you. They will usually come in the form of your friends.

Most of us do not know what we are doing with our lives.

~Pumua~

Not everyone deserves to know you the way you let them.

Be very aware of who you invite for a seat at your table.

Some of your 'friends' will pick, pick, pick from you until you have nothing left. And they will never give anything back.

Life awaits you.
Climb on board and suit up.
Or not...

My heart is exceedingly heavy with words. My mind is louder than roaring thunder and in all this chaos, perhaps, lays the solution to world peace.

You do not have to stay. Breathe.

Treat yourself kindly, softly, sweetly. You deserve it

Do not let your feelings for anyone cloud your ability to communicate what you truly think

Do not go searching for something if you know it will make you sad, cry, angry.

For every time I have tried to run away from my roots, they have pulled me back. Like roots do. I am forever grateful.

Kenyan and Proud.

Everyone you meet, regardless of their status, is still human.
DO NOT PANIC.

Celebrity status.

Respect everyone regardless of class, race, gender, sex, tribe. No one on this earth is above another.

Make love the driving force for everything that you do.

Not everything requires your reaction. Some things are just not your business. Never forget.

When you do something, do it passionately. Vagueness gives way to laziness.

Do not let social media take over your life, you don't need to see what everyone is up to. It is honestly none of your business. Never Forget.

You do not owe it to anyone to prove that you are living a good life. It is no one's business. Never Forget.

I am both delicate and coarse, gentle and vicious, I am the healer and the patient.

CONT. PAGE 142:

...unless it's Rihanna.

Thank you to all the women who have been my big and small sisters. Who have loved me, listened to me and held me out of self-destruction.

Thank you to all the women that met me halfway and guided, caressed, and raised me out of loneliness and untimely death.

Thank you to my mother who always made me laugh when tears was all I knew. For teaching me that there will always be more to life than the eye meets. I have found both father and mother in you.

Thank you to my father who has listened to understand rather than to respond. For teaching me passion, drive and motivation. I have found both father and mother in you.

Printed in Great Britain
by Amazon